mr. west

WESLEYAN UNIVERSITY PRESS   MIDDLETOWN, CONNECTICUT

WEST

sarah blake

WESLEYAN POETRY

Wesleyan University Press
Middletown CT 06459
www.wesleyan.edu/wespress
2015 © Sarah Blake
All rights reserved
Manufactured in the United States of America

Wesleyan University Press is a member of the Green Press Initiative. The paper used in this book meets their minimum requirement for recycled paper.

Excerpt in "Gaze" on pp. 89–91 from Catie Rosemurgy, "Variorum," in *The Stranger Manual.* Copyright © 2010 by Catie Rosemurgy. Reprinted with the permission of The Permissions Company, Inc., on behalf of Graywolf Press, Minneapolis, Minnesota, www.graywolfpress.org.

Excerpts in "The Fallible Face" on pp. 28–30 from Emmanuel Levinas, *Ethics and Infinity* (Pittsburgh, PA: Duquesne University Press, 1995), 86, 92; and *Totality and Infinity* (Pittsburgh, PA: Duquesne University Press, 1969), 75, 178, 199. Reprinted by permission of the publisher.

Library of Congress Cataloging-in-Publication Data
Blake, Sarah (Poet)
   [Poems. Selections]
   Mr. West / Sarah Blake.
     pages cm. — (Wesleyan Poetry series)
   Includes bibliographical references.
   ISBN 978-0-8195-7517-3 (cloth: alk. paper) —
   ISBN 978-0-8195-7518-0 (ebook)
  I. Title.
  PS3602.L3485A6 2015
  811'.6—dc23

               2014035803

5 4 3 2 1

This project is supported in part by an award from the National Endowment for the Arts.

ART WORKS.

National
Endowment
for the Arts
arts.gov

FOR kanye AND FOR noah

CONTENTS

THE FALLIBLE FACE

DEAR DONDA

DEAR KANYE

HYBRID

mr. west

MTV.com reported: At the end of his speech, West touched briefly on his mother's death and how he isn't scared of anything because he feels as though everything has been taken away from him. "I have no mother, no grandmothers, no girlfriend, no daughter, and I lived with a woman my whole life," he said.

Kanye is 33. If he were Jesus, he would die this year, and be resurrected.

I can't unthink this thought.

He said he had considered suicide, but found his life to be that of a soldier's,
"a soldier for culture."

Some men are kept alive by fighting.

I don't want this for you, Kanye.

To the right of the article is a video clip of an interview.

". . . both me and George express ourselves with our truest, our truest vision . . ."

Kanye's bottom teeth distract me.

If I ever questioned whether the diamonds were there,
they're there.

You're all kinds of beautiful.

And if that's not a word I can use, you're
resplendent, numinous, healthy.

I am two months pregnant.

Monday this premiere, Tuesday this article, Wednesday
my first ultrasound, with my child's boneless arms in motion.

A memory I didn't know I could have.

Thursday I write—If I have a daughter, you can hold her. A son, too.

The two of you, tied to this week in my life.

jesus walks

KANYE WEST, "Jesus Walks," line 6 of verse 1

HA HA HUM

In the chorus of one of my favorite songs are three throat-clearing
     sounds—
sometimes depicted as *Ha Ha Hum*
on lyrics websites such as azlyrics.com, lyricstime.com, and
     anysonglyrics.com.

A sound we make when we talk with the mouths of Jews.
          Channukah, l'chaim, chutzpah.
Voiceless fricative.

Russians have a letter for it. In block, an x, in Cyrillic, two c's back to
     back.
In the words, good, *chorrosho*, and bad, *plocho*.
They have other letters I love, for *sh, tss, sht, szh, yoo*.

The sound Kanye makes—it's not unlike the French r.
How my name falls back into the mouth like it's collapsing.
          Sa-cha.

In Russian, the r would roll, as when my great-grandmother said her
     name,
as when my great-grandfather called to her.
My name means *princess* in Hebrew.

Kanye's means *the only one* in Swahili.

A language once written in Arabic script, now written with letters like
    ours.

Switched in the 1800's. Trying for sounds like *nz* and *nd*, to begin
    words.

The mouths we speak with are hidden by our other mouths.

HEARTBREAK

The couple, who have dated on and off since 2002, got engaged over a lobster and pasta dinner during a vacation on the island of Capri in August 2006.

How does *People* magazine know this?

I hate to say things look like butterflies, but what should I say—the
    island
looks like motion? Like a liver?
It's an island.
You proposed to her and it looks like a butterfly.

The Italian map, covered in via, via, via. The Italian mountain. Citrus
    and gulls. I have never been to Italy, let alone to Capri. And I have
    never been to an island so small.

When the *New York Times* reporters write about *808s & Heartbreak*,
    they write how it came after "▮▮▮▮▮▮▮▮▮▮" with the death
    of his mother in late 2007 and, in early 2008, breaking up with his
    fiancée.

They don't name her. Alexis Phifer.

If Alexis is the woman in "Heartless," in the video, thank you
for covering her dress in stars.

I have planned my wedding—sent the invitations, tasted all the cakes,
    bought my dress, named for its sweetheart top, and sparkling. My
    mother has RSVP'd.

I got engaged in the courtyard of a museum in Philadelphia—
    Museum of
Archaeology and Anthropology.
Mummies resting
behind us, and sculptures from China.

The past pushes us.

I lament what you have lost even if you do not still love her.

I think of all the coves of Capri—Cala del Lupinaro, Cala del
    Rio, Cala di Mezzo, Cala Spravata, Cala Marmolata, Cala di
    Matermania. And Kapros, meaning wild boar.

LIKE THE POEMS DO

I ask,

    "Who's that?"

and Noah answers,

    "Mos Def."

    "Is Kanye rapping like Snoop Dogg there?"

    "No. His jaw is wired shut."

Another song,

    "Is that Common?"

    "Yes. They're friends. They're both from Chicago."

Noah's been listening

to rap since middle school. He used to make tapes

off the radio and listen to them until they broke.

I grew up saying, I listen to everything but country

and rap.

Recently, I spent another evening researching Kanye.

This time

about his 2004 debut album, *College Dropout*.

"Through the Wire" came out fast, without permission for the sample
   of Chaka Khan's "Through the Fire."

I tell Noah. We're on our computers,
across the room.
He pulls up Khan's song; I pull up Kanye's music video.

The room is a mess of sound.

I tell Noah how Kanye kisses his hand, places it
on a larger-than-life poster of Khan.

Is there a poem of Kanye as a teenager, loving
the woman who sings, too,
"I'm Every Woman"?

A smaller poster in his smaller room.

Noah with posters of Erykah Badu and Lauryn Hill,
if he were the sort of boy to have posters.

Noah and I move to the bedroom soon,
and every night. Noah lets me
                        bring Kanye in,
knows our life has room for all of it.

CON MOTO

While swallowing a prenatal vitamin before bed, I'm watching an
    MTV interview
with Rick Ross about how
you taught him to see music in colors.

He calls you *Ye*, pronounced yay, dropping *Kan*.

Musical terms, held onto from Italian, found on printed music, begin
    with *con*
because they begin with
with.

Con espressione, con moto, become, informally,
*espressione, moto, spirito, affetto, dolore, forza, gran, molto, fuoco,
larghezza, slancio, sordino, anima, brio, amore.* Shook free.

And we should love our own sounds.
Feeling, movement, spirit, affect, sadness, force, great feeling, much
    feeling, fire,
broadness, enthusiasm, muted tone, feeling again, and vigor, and
    tenderness

or love.

Another connection between you and Italy, between you and music.
    Another
way to say beautiful things that I have learned tonight.

If bellies stirred before babies were big enough, mine'd be kicking.

JESUS WALKS

This poem could start, "I love you," instead of ending there.
It could start, "Music."

The key to this poem is connecting this sentence,

▬▬▬▬▬▬▬▬▬▬▬▬▬▬▬▬▬▬

from the lyrics of Kanye's "Jesus Walks"

to this sentence,

Show 'em the wounds
from a *making of* video that follows
the making of the third music video
for "Jesus Walks."

Kanye said, after the first two videos, "I still felt like I didn't have the
hood, and that's what Jesus walks for, it's for the hood."

I can think, have thought, of great line breaks for that quote. Already
had to think of punctuation.

The man who said, "Show 'em the wounds," is, I imagine, a friend of
Kanye's. But Kanye's not around for this:

"I'm here with my n****, Romeo, looking smooth and shit. You know what I'm saying. Official, n****. How many times you got shot?"

"Nine," he's grinning and lifts up his shirt.

"Nine times goddamnit, and he ain't even no rapper, bitch." Pause. "I'm with my other n****," the man to his left, "how many times you got shot, n****? Tell 'em."

"Five times."

"Show 'em the wounds. Show 'em the wounds, show 'em the wounds." And he adds, "I ain't never got shot but my n****s did."

Stars all across my paper. Stars when I look at something blindingly beautiful. When I fall. When I first learn of stars.

Someone on the production crew yells out, "Come on in pigeon holders." Someone says, "I got dirt and blood standing by."

Many voices behind Kanye's repeat, "Jesus walks."

An actor—the one lit on fire for the video, the one carrying a cross big enough to carry him—says to the camera, "I hope people take it the right way."

My favorite music video of the three has this man in it.

Maybe for the fire behind Kanye that rises and recedes in that hallway like the breath.

Maybe because when the police cut open a pack of cocaine in the trunk of a car filled with packs of cocaine, a dove comes out, shaking powder from its head. I count at least fifteen flying from the trunk.

A woman sings that she wants Jesus with the fullest lips I've seen in years, a voice like no woman I know.

I believe in her, in Kanye.

But what is it when I believe bullets leave the shapes of stars?

Kanye, if only I could write a poem for you and not about you.

THE WEEK KANYE JOINED TWITTER

We find there are fewer dinosaurs
when we learn how the skulls age.
Shifting horns, bones that thin
and smooth, holes that form like
some desires do. Changes we
couldn't anticipate, knowing mostly
our simple, fusing domes.

                You begin tweeting.
I learn about your suits, videos,
jets, pillows, the new words you
picked up overseas. You take
a picture of your diamond
and gold teeth. You make a joke
about a crown so lovely I see
it on nymphs in daydreams.

                Sometimes I see
my curly head of hair outlined in
the morning dark and think I'm
the lovechild of actresses and lions.
But today I see the functionality
of my face and not whether
I'm beautiful. I'm so very animal.
I remember and flare my nostrils.

KANYE'S DIGESTIVE SYSTEM

This I taught to a sixth grader—

> *mouth, esophagus, stomach, small intestine, large*
> *intestine, rectum, anus*

—but there's so much more to it than that.

The bile from the liver.

The sections of the small intestine—
> *duodenum, jejunum, ileum.*

The sections of the large intestine—
> *ascending colon, transverse colon, descending colon.*

And some go so far as to note the *sigmoid colon.*

Wikipedia says,
> of this in particular,
> > "normally lies within the pelvis,
> but on account
> > of its freedom of movement
> > > it is liable to be displaced"

> > > *Oh god, the uneasy organs.*

All the sphincter muscles (just like the ones in our eyes).

All the peristalsis.

Even a vestigial organ.

I love the digestive system. The bits about how long the small intestine is.

The small intestine in an adult human measures on average
about 5 meters (16 feet), with a normal range of 3–7 meters.

It can measure around 50% longer at autopsy
                                        because of the loss of smooth
muscle tone
            after death.

How they will go on to say,
                That's the height of a giraffe!
                            The length of a Humpback Whale calf
at birth!

The length of the letters individually undone in this very book!
                .   *The length*
                                                    of my
                                                    cooing for
                                                    Kanye!

Cooooooooooooooooooooooooooooooooooooooooooooooooooooooooooooooooooooooooooooooooooooooooooooooo

Kanye must know, from his year in China, that there,
the heart is not what controls love.

It is the stomach, the gut,

                    that which moans in the night.

SEEING KANYE

Along the Juniata, the gray stones,
gray squares in the grass,
keep the hills from the road, keep them
where they are.

When we pass the stones,
like the Earth's stitches,
I know we're about to see a rock face
following a bend in the road,
where the strata bend like sound waves.

It's clear God is below the Earth, not above—
his head, giant frame for the planet—
and he makes a sound that makes the Earth.

But first I thought of Kanye's head
singing, singing, singing into that rock.

the fallible face

KANYE WEST, "Through the Wire," line 6 of verse 2

MYTHIC

The world's on the back of a turtle, on the back of a turtle, on the back
  of a turtle,

on the back of Kanye.

Eve gave Kanye the apple—after Kanye was formed of dust from the
  ground.

Kanye was raised by a nymph and not eaten by his Titan father.

With a giant axe, Kanye separated the murky Yin and clear Yang.

Kanye once grew from the ocean and reached the clouds in the sky.

And Kanye almost died in a car accident,

                                        so he became a star.

GOD CREATED NIGHT AND IT WAS NIGHT

Let there be Kanye at the wheel of a black SUV.
Let Kanye fall asleep.
Let the SUV hit another car with another man.
Let that man's legs break and be broken.
Let Kanye be trapped in the car.
Let there be the men that cut him out.

And there was evening and there was morning.

Let Kanye's mother and girlfriend arrive.
Let the women take care of him.
Let Kanye see his face.
Let the doctor reconstruct his face.
Let Kanye have the breath of life.
Let Kanye lie that he had not fallen asleep.

And there was evening and there was morning.

Let Kanye tell the truth.
Let Kanye's jaw be wired shut.
Let Kanye write a song.
Let Kanye sing it through that wire.

Let the song reach over all the earth.

Let lights in the firmament of the heavens to give light upon Kanye.

Bring forth Kanye according to his kind.

KANYE'S SKELETAL SYSTEM

206 bones, filled with marrow, connected
by tendons, ligaments, fitted in joints,
divided into axial and appendicular skeletons.

Bones break, fracture. They bruise. Sometimes,
kissing contusions.

> The Googled images for this show
> scans and x-rays of knees, and couples kissing,
> and pictures of Rihanna with Chris Brown.

Oh god, fact-checker.

Kanye has broken his bones.
But no matter how many places the skull
is broken, it's only one bone breaking.

First, a baby will have a skeleton completely
of cartilage.

In the fourth month of pregnancy, it begins to turn to bone.

And then I'll hold onto those bones forever.

Kanye, I could tell you so many more things about the bones.

I could tell you to drink your milk.

I could imagine you in the 80's "got milk?" ads.

That ad campaign began in 1993.

Fact-checker, please.

You're no better. What are you really thinking?

Kanye, did your mother, in her hands,
hold your broken face?

So swollen.
Could she?

THE FALLIBLE FACE

featuring Emmanuel Levinas

1

While firemen worked to get Kanye out,

he talked with his mother on the phone,
apologized for getting himself hurt.

2

The airbag had not deployed and his head had smashed against the
    steering wheel.
His mother got on a plane.

*there is first the very uprightness of the face, its upright exposure, without
    defense*

He was swollen.
He was indistinguishable.

this gaze is precisely the epiphany of the face as a face

His mother wrote how she controlled her expressions,
how she told his girlfriend how to behave.

the epiphany of the face is ethical

Women are familiar with how not to scare
someone who's in danger.

3

The plastic surgeon was a bit of eye candy
his mother wrote.

the face . . . formulates the first word

It might be love, or attraction, or
humanity.

4

Kanye, you must have a relationship with your reflection I can't
    understand.
To structure, to surgery, to form.

in the access to the face there is certainly also an access to the idea of God

How did they put you together again?
How did you feel when someone saw you who didn't know

you had ever looked like someone other
than yourself?

in the access to the face there is certainly also an access to the idea of God

The metal plate in your chin follows the bone.
The metal plate in your chin might ache.

5

Regardless of his face, Kanye is not always treated like a man.

THIS IS NOT THE FIRST TIME I'VE WONDERED

My favorite part of Donda West's *Raising Kanye* is from the chapter "Through the Wire: The Accident," when she sits at Kanye's bedside contemplating the attractiveness of the doctor, saying even that Billy Dee and Denzel Washington could not compare.

I want to spend my poem smiling.

> *Billy Dee, Donda? Lando Calrissian of* Star Wars? *Yes!*

But all I can think is, where is your father, Kanye?

> *Where is he?*
> *Where is he?*
> *Where is he?*

IN SONG

After the accident, Kanye West wrote, produced, and recorded a song.

"Through the Wire."

As the title suggests, Kanye rapped every word through his wired-shut jaw.

The first verse says:

Recently, Kanye compared himself to Emmett Till again.

On one website they explain: "discussing the VMA incident . . . he compared the backlash he faced to the murder of Emmett Till, the Chicago teenager who was killed for whistling at a white woman in Money, Mississippi."

People have been outraged, but Kanye must

feel a connection to this boy. And because of Kanye,

Emmett's story is on the internet again and again. 65 years later.

Kanye knows what appropriation is.

SO KANYE TRANSFORMED HIMSELF, PRODUCER TO SUPERSTAR

What do I know about being saved?

In one video game I watch Noah play,
he points his gun at his friend and shoots him to heal him.

My grandfather died despite treatment.
My mother's treatment did everything it should.

And I've never been in danger. I've hardly ever
been on high balconies or rooftops.

But Kanye's been at risk. In an interview, he was asked,

"Given that you had a near-death experience as you recount on 'Through
the Wire,' what are your beliefs on death? Reincarnation?"

He answered, "I feel like I'm here for a reason."

Why, Kanye? What's the reason?

Kanye said, "I don't believe in reincarnation. Sometimes I wonder if I
believe in heaven. I know I believe in Jesus."

I know you believe angels are with you.
This was not your first car accident.

My grandfather was never in car accidents
though he was legally blind in one eye.

An instance of saving I failed to notice?

My grandfather believed. He looked at the stars as proof
long after he stopped going to synagogue.

Kanye understood his belief—"I think 50% because it was instilled in me.
That's what we call on."

50% because you were saved?
What is it about being saved?

The best I know about saving is from childhood.
Jesus resurrected. Moses parting the sea. A Holocaust survivor.

Or one friend who refused to wear her seatbelt
because a relative lived when he didn't wear one.

Miraculous survival. Shock tumble through the air.
And I thought my friend was unreasonable.

I don't know how to be shaken,
to embrace a new belief,

but Kanye does.

dear donda

KANYE WEST, "Hey Mama," line 17 of verse 1

ADVENTURES

5 year anniversary of Katrina already.

I remember Bush reading a story to a classroom of children and not leaving. The book upside down.

Do I want to believe that?

No, that was after the planes flew into the World Trade Center.

On NBC, Kanye spoke out. I watched this clip over and over. He looks like he's going to cry. He says, "George Bush doesn't care about Black people," and they change who the camera's on.

They moved to Chris Tucker, stumbling over every scripted word.

Then, on ABC, an interview, "I'm working—I'm working off the cusp here. I'm working off the top of my mind. I'm not reading the teleprompter. I'm letting—I'm speaking from the heart, and that thing got dialed up and typed—typed into the heart. And that was that."

"Do you think it was fair?" asked the interviewer. But that wouldn't be my first question.

How does your heart work?

What else in the body could be the teleprompter?

The internet winds around. Not too many links before I find an interview between Larry King and Dr. Jan Adams, the cosmetic surgeon who operated on Kanye's mother the day before she died.

Adams went on the show to formally announce that he would
not partake in the interview at the wishes of the West family.

I'm disgusted by him because I've begun to love
your mother.

I'm working in the darkness between her teeth. I'm
reading
the measurements of her skull which is an excuse
to put my fingers in her hair.

She dedicated a whole chapter of her memoirs, *Raising Kanye*, to what he said about Bush and Katrina, to their trip to Houston. They brought Halloween masks to the children. And fifteen furnished homes for fifteen families for one year.

Though no one reported on this. Not one Houston Chronicle article.

Kanye had said, in that NBC clip, "I've even
been shopping before

even giving a donation, so now I'm calling
my business manager
right now to see what's—what is the biggest
amount I can give."

What is the biggest amount so that how
much remains?

I can't look up something like that.

A number I can't imagine.

After the earthquake in Haiti, Noah and I
donated $20 at Wegman's
and our cashier told us it was the largest
donation all day.

In one verse, in 2007, Kanye raps, " ███████████████████ ███████," and I would guess he dreams about Katrina.

About making a song, Kanye said, "I think about how people will react when they hear this. I think about how they will react to a certain point in the song. So, you know, a lot of time I try to build it up like an adventure."

And he does. And they are.
And I can imagine the water beginning to enter the house.

KANYE'S CIRCULATORY SYSTEM

upon the two-year anniversary of the death of my grandfather Allen

The blood helps because the heart helps because the electricity moves us.

Kanye, my circulatory system looks like yours. So you too have a soft
   vein
too big for your temple, a pulse in your thumb. You're still losing your
   mother.

One reporter called your mother's death " ███████████████████."
I apologize for him. He thinks, maybe, two years is a long time.

Last year, in Princeton, I tutored a sixth grader in every subject. As he
   learned
the systems of the body, I did too, beginning with the diagram of the
   heart.

What new words did you learn then? What new procession of breath
did you practice when I was teaching a boy how to say vena cava and
   aorta,

when I drew hearts on a chalkboard for him, day after day, and erased,
with my finger, the holes for the pulmonary veins to come in, to

fill the left atrium with the blood we could not draw? You recorded a
    song.
I'd love if you'd recorded a song. I almost forget again that your heart

looks like mine. You've heard the pulse in your ears then. You know
wush is not a foolish way to describe it. You miss her and I miss him but

surely I cannot say if, when you think of death, you, Kanye, think of the
    heart.

I WANT A HOUSE TO RAISE MY SON IN

1

I feel common.
There are people who want the house I want.

And if my desires are not unique,
what is?

A combination of my desires and my face
and the mud in the yard I don't yet have?

2

It's the worst time to be feeling this way,
when my legs are getting caught
on chairs and other places
I try to leave.

My hips just aren't able to hold myself
together anymore, so ready to bear

his terrible head—as when terrible
was used to describe God and Godly
everything.

3

I can hardly make it through.
Sleep comes and bends
my hands into positions of habit,
pinching the fluids that should move
like little fish through my wrists,
and shit. Shit. If I were my hand,
I'd be drowned. My hand is one
more part of me, maybe the last,
to realize I'm deathly ill, in that,
I could die from this.

4

I have made Noah promise he will save me over the boy
if it came to that.

I've told no one this.

It is my one non-maternal act, my one feeling
that reminds me of the selfish child I was
when I thought how I would have spit and peed
on the Torah if I'd been a child in the Holocaust,
if it would have saved me,
which, only as an adult do I understand,
could not have saved me.

I think I will be damned, killed, struck,
for not only admitting these betrayals,
but writing them down.

I'm afraid I will be a horrible mother because
I am a horrible woman.

5

Can I write anything after that?
Can the poem continue?
Can I return to my love for my son?

Can I tell how I imagine burying my nose
in his soft, small belly,
how I imagine making him the best room,
the best crib and chest of drawers?

One day we will redecorate his room as
he wants. And we
will play basketball in the driveway

at the house—
the house I want so badly for him.

6

I lie in bed, as I can hardly leave it now,
and read books about Kanye. I page through
the one about Kanye's Glow in the Dark tour.
It reminds me of my son's bones, glowing white
in ultrasounds, in a more wretched darkness.

Donda made it seem easy in her memoir.
To love Kanye. To unconditionally love him.
She even knew he was a boy. In utero.

My son remains my mystery.
The ultrasounds revealing him
well-formed. No clubbed foot.
Black stomach means he can
swallow. Black bladder means
his kidneys are working. Heart

can be seen in detail, valves,
deep inside me. His hair grown.
His nose like mine. Arms, legs,
moving. Everything moving.

7

I want to lie in the grass of my yard with my son.
Every part of him in the sun. Every part of each of us.

ON NOVEMBER 10TH, 2007, DONDA WEST DIED

On November 10th, 2008, you were between shows. November 9th, Dublin, Ireland. November 11th, London, England.

By ferry and car, the journey from Dublin to London takes about eight hours.

By plane, about an hour.

I have to imagine you flew. But maybe not. Maybe you spent two hours, three hours, on a ferry.

> *The journey between two points is such a straight line.*

Maybe you needed to be on the Irish Sea. The blue of it. The blue looks miserable.

The very shape of the sea is like a face, mourning, gagging on a moan.

And it must be salty, like all seas.

Though for a sea to leave cliffs instead of beaches.

> *That tells me it's killed its fair share of mothers.*

The Irish stop clocks at the time of death. They stay with the body day and night until the burial. They recite poems. They sing. They cry and drink. They kiss the dead body.

Given the autopsy, at least some of these, you were unable to do.

But the first anniversary of a death. I know it.

We sometimes burn a *yahrzeit* candle. It burns for 24 hours, or 26, or 3 days, more. It's white and burns in a tall glass so you don't have to worry about leaving an open flame over night.

Do you worry about your house burning down?

You spent the nights around the anniversary of your mother's death on a stage that looked like the universe.

Planets. Shooting stars. A galaxy—pink and perfect.

You were glowing in the dark. And you were black in the dark.

And a monster came on stage to eat you.

To gobble you up. As mothers say.

DEAR DONDA

1

I wonder what you would think, seeing the dead white women in
    Kanye's "Monster" music video.
I wonder what you would think of me, vitreous, near translucent in my
    skin.

When you thought of white women, I wonder if you thought of *Under
the Tuscan Sun.*

2

This isn't the time for a racist joke.
It's my fear coming out.
That I'm growing to be a worthless voice.

3

I had a professor who read an early draft of "Kanye's Skeletal System."
He didn't believe you would hold Kanye's face, not because he was hurt,
    but because

you weren't a caring woman. Something about how much money you
    had,
something about dying after plastic surgery.

My giant belly in front of me made it easier to sit and fight
than leave the room. *You're being racist.*
And I told him you had a PhD in English. I knew he'd be surprised,
but I wish I hadn't told him.

So many worthwhile women in this world.
Black or not. Mother or not. Rich or not. Plastic surgery or not. Dead
    or not.

4

Another man tells me I haven't made enough of your death.

Well, I miss you, the idea of you I can carry around after reading
"███████████████████████████████."

That's all I have to say about it.

When I wanted to put my fingers in your hair, I wasn't saying, *Can I
    touch it?*
I was saying caress.

RUNAWAY

On Kanye West's website is a still frame from his movie—Kanye carry-
ing a woman from an explosion filled with as many pinks as yellows
and oranges (and a red like a flaming heart, if a burnt thing red-
dened, if light were pushed through the skin).

Just below it, there's a Twitter feed. It shows three tweets at a time.
Any tweet hashtagged with
Runaway, runaway, RunAway, etc.

The first tweet when I visit today:
"I txt my Mom & told her I love her, she said I coulda came
downstairs to say that... I dnt think she noticed I was gone
LMFAO! #RunAway"

I didn't understand at first. So literal. So misplaced. She had actually
run away. From her mother.
And she was laughing about it.

As if,
in front of Kanye.

aftermath

. . . taking a 15 second blip the mdeia have successfully painted the image of the "ANGRY BLACK MAN' The King Kong theory.

KANYE WEST on Twitter, 6:22 a.m., Sept. 4, 2010,

via web; retweeted by 100+ people

THREE MONTHS, TO THE DAY, BEFORE
TAYLOR TURNED TWENTY, BUT KANYE

I'm not mad. I read on your site about how you spoke to Taylor's mother, heard your mother in her. You used over forty exclamation marks and I think that's how America needs to be spoken to. America can be found pining for you in her bedroom. Your hair like an Aztec god's. Your biceps like the end of days. This moment, on YouTube, viewed millions of times. Taylor's little ketchup mouth.

I could see that Beyoncé had to smile.   Even I could see that.

AFTERMATH

The world that opened,
as if Kanye were Hades and Taylor, Persephone,
and we all believed in the Greek myths and traveled back
in time to save her, to have our say, shake a fist.

I mean, everyone, just everyone, asks if I'll write a poem
about the 2009 MTV Video Music Awards.

What deep hole in the Earth is this?

HATE FOR KANYE

As found on: youtube.com/watch?v=9d8S_9PZ56M, a clip (viewed 6,305,621 times) about the Taylor Swift incident.

Comments time-stamped as of 5:30 pm on November 7, 2010 (over a year after the incident).

3 hours ago ▓▓▓▓▓▓▓ :   @▓▓▓▓▓▓▓ not only is he a freakin pubic headed idiot, I bet his_ breath smells like shit . . . dumb ass afro!!!

21 hours ago ▓▓▓▓▓▓▓▓▓▓▓ :   @▓▓▓▓▓▓ -damn right! Kayne is an arrogant racist prick! It's funny_ that your so politically correct calling him "afro american" because he would probably call you a cracker or honkey or something like that, and he would get away with it. kanye west is an overall mean ignorant asshole!

2 days ago ▨▨▨▨ : I hope_ Chuck Norris kills Kanye West.

3 days ago ▨▨▨▨▨▨▨ : I'm not saying someone should beat the living_ crap out of Kanye West, but I'm not not saying it either.

1 day ago ▨▨▨▨▨ : @▨▨▨▨▨▨ i'll do it for free man just tell me where his ass live's & he's got a ass kicking coming his way & i hate kanye he's a fucking punkass bitch who's never have pussie since pussie had him motherfucker need's to do kkk a favor & kill himself & no i'm not racist or a member of the_kkk but kanye disgrace's black's everywhere & forever is to be label as a nigger as only nigger do that shit a black person doesn't.

3 days ago ▨▨▨ : K West . . . Your a dick you_ faggot black asshole..your a disgrace to not only blacks but to all Americans . . . get the fuck out of here you morron!!

3 days ago ▨▨▨▨ : fuck you kanye_

4 days ago ▨▨▨▨ : kanye is the most uneducated_ human(?) being ever!

4 days ago ▓▓▓▓▓▓▓▓: Kanye is a fucking douchebag little bitch he only went on stage to get some camera time because he never wins any awards cause he has no fans exept the black homos_ that are actually stupid enough to believe anything that comes out of his big mouth.

2 weeks ago ▓▓▓▓▓▓▓▓▓: is Kanye_Dead yet???? DAMN I was sooo HOPING

2 weeks ago ▓▓▓▓▓▓▓: What an absolute piece of shit racist fuck stick he is. Some one should take him out and shoot him to make_ the world a better place!

A DAY AT THE MALL REMINDS ME OF AMERICA

Recently, my 14-year-old sister was approached at the mall to see if she'd be interested in working at Hollister, or Abercrombie and Fitch, or American Eagle. I can't remember.

She's that beautiful. And with the mall's lights all around her—I can only imagine.

Yet on Facebook, one of her friends calls her a loser. More write, "I hate you."

I wonder if Kanye knows that these girls are experimenting. As with rum. As with skin, all the ways to touch it.

My day at the mall begins with a Wild Cherry ICEE and an Auntie Anne's Original Pretzel. A craving.

I pass women who you can tell are pregnant, and I know we all might be carrying daughters.

The mall is so quiet. The outside of the Hollister looks like a tropical hut, like the teenage girls should be sweating inside.

No one's holding doors for me yet, but they will as I take the shape of my child.

And if my child has a vicious tongue, it will take shape lapping at my breast.

TAYLOR DOESN'T SPEAK OUT AGAINST RACISM

People are upset because Kanye's talking about Taylor again.
He apologizes without apologizing. He speaks out. He rehashes. But
    this time

he says, "Taylor never came to my defense at any interview . . ."
So the media writes as if little girls all over the country are upset
    again.

But I've read the comments and I think it's some of Taylor's white
    knights
who keep up with these articles. Who else says "waste a shell on this
    POS"?

I'm starting to blame her, too. She could sing a song about it
that makes a little more sense. She could say, *Don't hate him.*

IT'S HARD NOT TO BE MOVED

I can tell—it's starting to get to Noah.

Often he's with me when I'm doing research.

Today I went to copy-paste a comment into an e-mail, and he stopped
    me,
said I needed to take both comments,
that it was *significant* that there were only two and this is what they
    said.

So this part is for Noah:

> http://www.411mania.com/music/news/164797/Kanye-West-To-Appear-
> On-Kardashian-Reality-Show.htm

> Comments (2)

> 1) Wow, Kanye looks mad fuckin lame in that pic. At least he [mostly]
> makes good music.

> Posted By: SS87 (Guest) on December 04, 2010 at 01:12 AM

> 2) fucking awesome!!!!....no, really...i hope he dies....i do, i hope he god-
> damn dies...fuck him, goddamn concieted hypocrit muther fucker...the

only ratings he will deliver is if he gets decapitated on live television dur-
ing half time of the super bowl...i'd actually watch that

and don't feed me any of your sympathetic bullshit...he's an untalented
con artist and racistthat deserves to be beaten with a hammer and thrown
screaming from a helicopter

Posted By: mikey (Guest) on December 04, 2010 at 04:21 AM

We're both still surprised at the racism and violence and hate.
We're full of fear

but that's not what fearsome means.

HATE IS FOR HITLER

my mother used to tell me.
So I said and say, I don't like . . . really don't like . . . can't stand . . .
My grandmother used to say it.

I wonder if Kanye's mother said it too.
Unconditional love
is what she speaks most about in her memoir.

I wonder if raised in a good family in Alabama
she picked up the same saying
my grandmother did

when she lived with her mother as one
of the oldest of six sisters and five brothers
in Philadelphia after the Depression.

All of my grandmother's friends went off to World War II.
She went to the dances for the servicemen, held them,
then followed the lists that were posted, lists of dead men.

How can these kids say they hate Kanye?
Why do they hate? Why is the word
in their mouths and out their fingers?

I think Kanye's like me,
and I think it's incomprehensible.
I think he and I and my mother and Donda West

are easily moved.
We enter into discourse thinking first,
love.

BECAUSE KANYE ISN'T KING KONG OR EMMETT TILL OR A N****

When I admire my small, white nose, I'm Taylor Swift.

Too, if I'm made of red candies and floral underwear,

if I spend a day descending all the stairways I can find.

It's one way to be a woman, a woman being a girl.

I could meet the many white knights, with their hands

around swords, their ears perked to the motion of men.

If I ever thought life was a whistle, I thought it twice.

dear kanye

KANYE WEST, "Power," line 13 of verse 2

MY SUMMER WITH KANYE

So many crickets, small and brown, so small, babies maybe, hardly in control, their jumps foolish and sweet.

My birthday this year was everything I wanted it to be. My mother and sisters came. We swam in the Hampton Inn's outdoor pool. We ate prepared foods from Wegman's.

That day, the *New York Times* ArtsBeat blog posted about a preview of Kanye's music video for "Power."

So much is false, and the voice of the viewer. *Is* Kanye imposing? *Is* the chain heavy? Do the women kneel *before* him? What does that look like? A woman apologizing? With some request?

The horns are not as devilish as they are the horns of dinosaurs, the Minotaur, an African gazelle, a god of the sea I imagine, the shapes of twisted arms, dark, twisted arms.

And there is no ceiling. The sky moves in the video.

Two weeks later, Kanye is quoted as saying, "I'm not trying to dive into anything unless I really, really think that I can marry this person. I look at this person and I say, 'This is how I want my daughter to be.'"

I'm thinking of babies, too.

WATCHING WEEKS

I am mother to the smallest baby.
Inside, fingernails grow this week.

So we bought our first video camera.

The language of documentation
comes to me immediately. "This is
what I'm working on. This is
your dad doing a dance for you."

I didn't mention Kanye. But
this week is no small week for him.
He premiered his 35-minute movie.
He compared his shots to Kubrick,
his acting to Tarantino. And he
explained his ideas on MTV as if
he were speaking to children.

This should be a week I commit
to grading 80 pages of student work,
but I can't help but sleep. 16 hours
one day. 14 another. I wake to eat.

My students ask me to play more
Kanye music videos during our class.
And I think we *could* put the label
"Phenomenon" above his name
in the center of the board. Follow
"Causes" to the left, "Consequences"
to the right. How many composition
lessons I could make about Kanye,
his music and life. If I felt up to it.

This week I try to feel the baby, still
hidden from us, from Noah's kisses.

I TRY NOT TO SEE MYSELF AS A MOTHER FIGURE

I imagine Kanye's hand on my stomach
because I've begun to imagine that everyone's
touching me through my clothes.

I was not one for fantasies,
but fantasizing makes me more of a woman.
If I see Kanye's teeth

in my bedroom, if I see him
with the head of a falcon, penis of a buck
(which I've never seen), or

if I see myself in his studio,
in his house, introduced to Jay-Z,
drinking what I can't drink—I am a fool.

I am encouraged to paint myself the fool.
Tattoo of Kanye's head on my hip.
Something to morph.

To humble me. Humiliate me.
If I can only see myself protecting Kanye,
am I even a woman?

DEAR KANYE,

I can't draw a parallel today between you and the branch I saw on the sidewalk. It wasn't like the tree branches here—it was like one you'd see on the beach, maybe only a New Jersey beach, but I think others, too. And it resembled an arm. That's what I remember thinking. And it wasn't the first time something on these sidewalks near my house reminded me of an arm or a hand. There's a leaf I remember distinctly. My mind is so quick to see these dead pieces of trees as lonely parts of the body. And my mind *tries* to connect this stone-gray arm to you. My mind sees that where the branch broke from the tree (if it is a branch at all and not chopped from the trunk), there is wood that curves together to the sidewalk in such a way that fingers might. And my mind asks if these are not the fingers that move freely in a dream and play some kind of music for you, or run along the top of your head in the manner of one who loves you. Are they not the fingers that begin to resemble your mother's?

I realize some days I shouldn't write about you.

AFTER DONDA DIED, KANYE DATED AMBER

The question all around the internet was,
Is Kanye West's Girlfriend Trashy?

Her birth name is Alyssa Audrey Rose Palmer.

On YouTube, the interviews are short and sometimes
raunchy as hell.

"I'm actually a virgin in my ass," she said.

In other videos, all the ones where her face is
front and center, and she's got blue lipstick, sunglasses
in the shapes of hearts,
or her bra out—

she's chewing gum. Like a cow,
I think, in my eighth grade science teacher's voice.

She licks her teeth while she's making points like,
"I don't have a stylist."
Something along the lines of *make sure they know*,
"I style myself."

Her interviewer responds,
"I live and die for that,"
in a voice I've heard on black sitcoms in the '90s.

Someone in the comments writes
to women who watch this video—like me—

"YO IF THERES ANY OTHA HOT_ CHICK LIKE THIS ONE holl-
laaa"

Do I respond?
Is *he* trashy?

Why do women watch this video of Amber?
Are they looking for the Kanye in her?

Girl, raised by her aunt, with a name as sunshine as hers—Mary
    Lakes.
Girl, Portuguese, Italian, African, Irish. Former
exotic dancer. Featured in music videos of Young Jeezy and Ludacris.

I remember hearing that she might marry Kanye in the Caribbean in
    January 2011.
I remember thinking, *Is she trashy as all get out, right on Kanye's
    arm?*

SUGE KNIGHT

Suge is pronounced like sugar without its -ar.
Liar turns lie. Color turns cull. Whisper, wisp.

In August 2005, Kanye hosted a party before the Video Music Awards.
    And Suge got shot there.

MSNBC reports:
        ambulance, fire and police officials swarmed
        the shooter was described *as black and wearing a pink shirt*
Giddy. Frivolous.
Treasure, trezh. Splendor, splend. Shiner, shine.

In March 2010, Suge is suing Kanye for money, but a car accident
    keeps him from his court date.

Perez Hilton reports
a quote from Knight's lawyer:
        Nobody likes Kanye West anymore.
        Even though he's still selling millions of records, everybody's
            sick of him.
Error, err. Geyser, guise. Razor, raise   blaze.

The bullet took the light from the front of the gun. The bullet took the
   light into the leg and bone.

I think Suge's alight with something like grief.
Can Kanye save him from something like that?

KANYE AS A QUANTUM PARTICLE YET TO BE OBSERVED

Is there room in a biography for what didn't happen?

> December 2010, Miami—Kanye's once-scheduled court date
> with Suge Knight.
> January 2011, Dominican Republic—his once-rumored
> wedding to Amber Rose.

Less than three hours to fly from one place to the other, to fly
over the Bahamas that fall like inch worms from Florida's peninsula,

to fly to a country that shares an island with Haiti, that nearly touches
Port Au Prince with its border like a series of shark fins.

How would their marriage have begun? Following such trouble,
the slow pulse of the Earth destroying the Earth. But then,

how funny if Suge's missing earring had ended up on Amber's finger.
Photos of her in the tabloids as she leaves a car, stands from a table.

If Kanye's life collided, collapsed. If he woke one morning
and, having made no decisions, all the possibilities came to be.

hybrid

WE LIVE THIS SHIT! WE EMBODY THIS
SHIT! WE WOULD IDE FOR THIS SHIT SO
YOU YOU CAN LIVE FOR THIS SHIT!

KANYE WEST, on Twitter, 2:05 p.m.,
Jan. 26, 2011, via web; retweeted by 50+ people

GOD'S FACE OVER GOLD

Kanye West has a god's face over gold.
But his eyes are like man's. His voice overflows.
So it must be his mouth, his tongue unrolled.
Kanye West has a god's face over gold.
I think he hears prayers when nights are cold.
He can't be a man when his heart's a rose.
Kanye West has a god's face over gold.
But his eyes are like man's. His voice overflows.

TWILIGHT: STARRING KANYE

The vampires are who everybody
wants in their movies right now, but who knows
what *new* creature we'll see ourselves kissing. I'm
thinking the next one won't idealize a
white man, but maybe those motherfucking
types go on forever. What monster

has such sparkling *black* skin? What monster
has sparkling black skin but everybody
can find him more man than motherfucking
beast, can still desire him, godlike, knows
it's safe for their sweet daughters to have a
cutout of him in their sweet bedrooms. I'm

not thinking of zombie Michael. I'm
thinking the black man can't be a monster
because he is one, because we won't let a
fantasy form around him. Everybody
has at least one dream where the city knows
it's in trouble. And it's the motherfucking

dreamer who has a foot on motherfucking
towers, people, and cars and shit. Or I'm
hoping I'm not the only one. God knows

there's room for one sweating, flexing monster
in my head. And it's everybody
else who's walking by and flickering a

bit on the street, just waiting for a
person like me to ask, "What monster
would you be? Land or sea? Could everybody
love you like that?" Somewhere on the street, I'm
yelling, "You can't make every monster
into sexy Halloween costumes." Kanye knows

why fantasy exists, and stories, knows
how to make women look dead and fill a
room with them. And he's called a monster.
I should be in love with motherfucking
Edward Cullen I guess. I guess I'm
a fool to love Kanye. And everybody

can just freak when "███████████████
███████████████████" too.

HYBRID

Kanye is Horus, or another Egyptian god.
He is a merman, a centaur, the Minotaur.

And less mythical, too—a zorse,
a sand sunflower, a Lonicera fly.

Kanye is half cannon, half ballet.
Half canonical, half prey.

Half my Man of Sorrows.
Half my son.

Half an idol for my son.
Half an idol of diamonds and gold.

Oh god,
Kanye is half what makes my heart.

GAZE

featuring Catie Rosemurgy

Most of the privilege has been off the page.

A white woman has privilege but not power.
A black celebrity has privilege but not power and also discrimination.

Has it in his hands, his hood, buried in the pavement against his face.

A white Jewish woman has privilege until she's traveling in France.

Then riots start. Schools and synagogues firebombed.

"Dirty Jew" written on a statue of Alfred Dreyfus in Paris in 2005.

What does hiding look like?
What does it look like today?

Most of the violence takes place off the page, as is always the case.

The ultimate test of the privilege: the violence.

A black celebrity has privilege as much as he doesn't have privilege.
Or not as much. Up and down. Plummeting. Pummeling. Depending.

A white Jewish woman gets privilege from her mother's Irish married
name. Except for all those signs.

No N****s, No Jews, No Dogs

No Irish, No Blacks, No Dogs

No Jews Allowed

No Irish Need Apply

If it weren't for the print on the signs.

For the most part, the violence is not on the page.

A white pregnant woman has privilege but also shortness of breath,
    also judgment.
My ring doesn't fit on my finger anymore.

"What did you think?" I asked her.
She shrugged, "Teen mom."
She smiled like I was her darling.

A black pregnant woman has privilege but worse judgment and also
    discrimination.

Still comfortable on her finger, impossible to swell out of, or we would
have all done that already.

In the Holocaust the barrel of a gun was shoved up the vagina of a
white pregnant Jewish woman and her baby was shot and so she was.
Is 70 years a long time?

For the most part, this page is not violent.

For the most part, this page is privileged.

A pregnant woman has privilege until the boys won't make room for
her to get off the bus.

But when I ask, they do. Another form of privilege. A birch tree I'm
peeling bark from, so I can make a boat, so I can get out of here,
so I can come back in the spring. So I'm asking.

And it sounds like, *Move. You have to move.*

TEETH

Do all the children's teeth come in like razors?

Noah's hurt face when our son bites.

Will Kanye stick his finger in his goddaughter's mouth?

Every washed finger on her gums.

Kanye's gold teeth are like toy soldiers for a little emperor tongue.

Or, welded together, the castle.

Moat inside his lower lip. My finger, the drawbridge.

If I could touch him there.

Does every mother remember the first tooth?

Milk tooth.

I run my tongue along the back of my own dull teeth.

One can lose attachment to weariness.

I understand. But in dreams, they are handsome again.

When teeth should not even be in dreams.

Why am I not flying? Why am I not covered in gold?

KANYE RAPS, "████████ ████████," PART I

Paris is most definitely Kanye.

Helen, then, is Kim Kardashian.

King Menelaus is a great number of men in America.

Achilles. I'm not sure yet who Achilles is.

Hera is Beyoncé.

Athena is Nicki Minaj.

Aphrodite is the night, which allows for things like this.

The Trojan War is the sex itself.

KANYE IS GLAMOROUS

OH "THE NEW BLACK???" SINCE BARACK IS PRESIDENT BLACKS
DON'T LIKE FUR COATS, RED LEATHER, AND FRIED CHICKEN ANY
MORE?! WHEN YOU TRULY UNDERSTAND CULTURAL SETTINGS,
BOUNDARIES, AND OUR MODERN DAY CASTE SYSTEMS, THEN YOU
CAN FEEL THE GLORY AND PAIN FROM THE DAYS OF KINGS IN
AFRICA TO THE NEW KINGS OF THE MEDIA.

There is something about fur, isn't there?

I remember the coats with fur-lined hoods, and my fashionable sister,
    and her faux fur,
how it touched her face and hair.

                                    I thought of how it would gather dust,
                                                              finely.

                          Because I think, often, how to keep a clean house.

In our house, when we moved in, we found old hat boxes with old
    hats, one leopard, like
Audrey Hepburn wore.

Then there are my ideas of Russia, all the white skin of the characters
    in Tolstoy's novels.
(Because I guess it *is* racial.) How often they would have touched fur.

Sometimes I cry that Anna Karenina isn't real.

Other times I remember she never abandoned her son.
There was no son.

Kanye mentioned the kings in Africa, and yes, them, too. Wearing
    cheetah, leopard, lion.
Mouths collapsed as if they once sung.

And Kanye designed fox fur backpacks for his fashion line, and the
    women carried them,
and the word, luxury, appeared over and over.

A fox neck wrap is 500 dollars, and if I wore only that,
I would be a sexy woman.

A shitty hunter, but a sexy woman.
Maybe not a mother at all.

I think about the fox that lives in the yards behind ours, and the
    neighbors, fearing for
their small dogs. My son, crawling in the grass.

An animal without skin is
a stranger animal.

As a girl, I drew women with foxes around their necks. One woman,
    her hand stroking
the red tail, her head distracted, the fox's head arranged toward her
    breast.
The fox's eye, a jewel?

I NO LONGER HAVE TO LOOK UP DATES
LIKE YOUR BIRTHDAY, JUNE 8, 1977

You held your 30th birthday party at a Louis Vuitton store. Fitting
for Kon the Louis Vuitton Don, a name
that follows your 2000 mixtape, your first.

People magazine waited outside your party, as I imagine
they always do. And you told them,
I'm in my 20s as we speak right now, but at midnight, I'll be 30. I'm
    already 30 in Japan and London and everywhere else.

Inside, Pharrell of The Neptunes and N.E.R.D., an overweight
    Mariah Carey,
Common, of course, and Rihanna in a wig.
And a cake, at least three feet long, with your signature bear on it,
his wild-colored eyes.

Another cake too, with your name spelled wrong, Kayne. Who doesn't
    know you?

After the party, 30,000 dollars of merchandise was missing. So says
    Hip Hop Crunch.
More people who want to write about you. The hundreds

of reviewers on Amazon, the commenters on YouTube, the bloggers, the
   magazines,
the poet.

And now you're 37.

KANYE RAPS, "████████ ████████████," PART 2

Achilles.

I couldn't see it before
because I'm Achilles.

Apollo, god of poetry,
light, music, and plague,

stuck an arrow in my heel.

Except
not yet.

We're not at the war's end.
There is time still

to utter and croon.

*

"'Runaway' Premieres in Los Angeles on October 18, 2010": See Kanye West on *Ellen.*

"Ha Ha Hum": See West's "Barry Bonds."

"Heartbreak": See *808s & Heartbreak* as Noah's Valentine's Day present for me in 2009.

"Heartbreak": See a $466 fee for a quote. See www.nytimes.com/top/reference/timestopics/people/w/kanye_west.

"Con Moto": See West interviewed by MTV in 2005. See him speak out against gay bashing, saying, "Not just hip-hop, but America just discriminates. And I wanna just, to come on TV and just tell my rappers, just tell my friends, 'Yo, stop it.'"

"Jesus Walks": See, between the two verses, the fourth line. See Channel Zero TV.

"Mythic": See creation myths. See October 23, 2002.

"God Created Night and It Was Night": See Genesis.

"The Fallible Face": See *Ethics and Infinity* and *Totality and Infinity* by Emmanuel Levinas.

"In Song": See lines five to eight of verse one. See lyrics blacked out throughout the book because permission to print could not be gained.

"In Song": See NewsOne.com, Breaking News for Black America.

"So Kanye Transformed Himself, Producer to Superstar": See the 2003 interview at HipHopSite.com.

"Adventures": See line nine of verse two of West's "Flashing Lights."

"Adventures": See George Bush tell Matt Lauer that West's comment during the Katrina fundraiser "was one of the most disgusting moments in [his] presidency."

"Kanye's Circulatory System": See public grief vs. private grief. See grieving.

"Kanye's Circulatory System": See another $4.66 fee for a quote. See www.nytimes .com/2010/01/03/arts/music/03kanye.html?_r=0.

"On November 10th, 2007, Donda West Died": See West's Glow in the Dark tour.

"Dear Donda": See not being able to get permission from the estate. See page 52 of *Raising Kanye* by Donda West.

"Three Months, to the Day, before Taylor Turned Twenty, but Kanye": See West at the 2007 BET Hip-Hop Awards, giving away his award for best video of the year to UGK and Outkast, who he thought were more deserving.

"Aftermath": See "pull a Kanye" on Urban Dictionary. See most of the definitions having to do with interrupting someone, but one saying "To be in need of Midol." Because emotional outbursts, asking for fairness, asking for things in general, is feminine. Because if you need to ask for something, you have less power. Because if you get emotional while asking for something, forget about it. See some old archetypes at work. See my hope that West's emotional outbursts are shifting things, saying men can be emotional in the public eye. See a future where the emotional is just the emotional, not tied to gender. See no display of emotion undermined.

"Hate for Kanye": See West leave the country in his response to America's reaction to the Swift incident. See a few weeks in Japan. See four months in Italy, interning at Fendi. See him come back, receive many Grammy nominations, and comment, "Good logic tells me 'smile Kanye,' the world likes you again."

"A Day at the Mall Reminds Me of America": See my two sisters. See my youngest. She's Chinese, adopted. I was 13 when my mother went to China and brought her home. See her like a daughter.

"Taylor Doesn't Speak Out Against Racism": See comments made at concerts.

"It's Hard Not to Be Moved": See the definition of fearsome: frightening, especially in appearance.

"My Summer with Kanye": See the blog post, "A Preview of Kanye West's 'Power':
'Apocalyptic in a Very Personal Way,'" at the *New York Times* ArtsBeat.

"My Summer with Kanye": See comments made on the radio.

"Watching Weeks": See West's music video for "Can't Tell Me Nothing" and the
music video Zach Galifianakis made for the same song, and discuss form vs. con-
tent. If I could include videos in this book, I would.

"I Try Not to See Myself as a Mother Figure": See Aziz Ansari's stand up about
meeting West and hanging out with him and Jay-Z: "Jay-Z was drinking vodka
he *makes*. How baller is that? Jay-Z's on the tab, and the money went back into
his own pocket."

"Suge Knight": See Suge Knight lose the case.

"God's Face over Gold": See West's musical performances on the episode of *Satur-
day Night Live* that aired on October 3, 2010.

"Twilight: Starring Kanye": See sestina. See line two of the chorus of West's "Mon-
ster." See Nicki Minaj have one of the best verses in hip hop's history.

"Hybrid": See the February 2006 Rolling Stone's cover. See West's BET perform-
ance of "Power." See West's "Runaway."

"Gaze": See Catie Rosemurgy's "Variorum" from her book, *The Stranger Manual.*

"Gaze": See my father-in-law, born before the end of World War II. See his mother,
choosing to get pregnant and bring a Jewish child into this world at a time
when Jews were being killed by the millions. See, I imagine, an incredible
amount of faith in herself as a mother, in her ability to provide. See how she was
right. See how that's incredible. If she hadn't, I wouldn't have my husband or
my son.

"Teeth": See Blue Ivy Carter, daughter of Jay-Z and Beyoncé.

"Kanye Is Glamorous": See Barack Obama calling West a jackass in 2009, and af-
firming his statement in 2012. See West's response in a 2010 *XXL* interview,
"He was trying to pass the healthcare bill. And if he said that to relate to the

room or lighten the room up and the whole mood, then I'd be more than happy to be the butt of all of his jokes if it in some way helps his overall mission."

"Kanye Raps, '███████████████████████'": See line three of verse two of West's "Way Too Cold."

"Kanye Raps, '███████████████████████'": See Evan McGarvey, who first said West was Paris.

"Kanye Raps, '█████████████████████'": See North (Nori) West, baby girl of Kardashian and West, born June 15, 2013. See Kardashian and West married on May 24, 2014.

ACKNOWLEDGMENTS

Sincere thanks to the editors of the following journals, who published many of these poems, often in earlier versions:

At Length: "After Donda Died, Kanye Dated Amber," "Kanye as a Quantum Particle Yet to Be Observed," "It's Hard Not to Be Moved," "Because Kanye Isn't King Kong or Emmett Till or a N****," "Jesus Walks," "I Want a House to Raise My Son In," "Dear Donda," "Runaway"

The Awl: "Ha Ha Hum," "Heartbreak," "Kanye's Circulatory System," "Seeing Kanye"

Barrelhouse: "Twilight: Starring Kanye," "Teeth," "Kanye Raps, ▇▇▇▇▇▇▇▇▇ ▇▇▇▇▇▇▇▇▇,' Part 1," "Kanye Raps, '▇▇▇▇▇▇▇▇▇▇▇▇▇▇▇,' Part 2"

Boston Review: "A Day at the Mall Reminds Me of America," "Three Months, to the Day, Before Taylor Turns Twenty, but Kanye," "'Runaway' Premieres in Los Angeles on October 18, 2010," "I Try Not to See Myself as a Mother Figure," "Suge Knight," "Kanye Is Glamorous," "Adventures"

Drunken Boat: "Kanye's Skeletal System," "My Summer with Kanye"

Fleeting Magazine: "The Week Kanye Joined Twitter"

#GOODLitSwerveAutumn: An Anthology of Independent Literature About Kanye West: "Con Moto," "In Song," "On November 10th, 2007, Donda West Died," "God's Face Over Gold"

JERRY: "Hate Is for Hitler," "I No Longer Have to Look Up Dates Like Your Birthday, June 8, 1977," "Hybrid"

Juked: "Kanye's Digestive System"

MiPOesias: "Like the Poems Do"

The Musehouse Journal: "Watching Weeks," "Taylor Doesn't Speak Out Against Racism"

The Northville Review: "Aftermath"

Sentence: "Dear Kanye"

Witness: "God Created Night and It Was Night," "The Fallible Face," "So Kanye Transformed Himself, Producer to Superstar"

"A Day at the Mall Reminds Me of America" was developed as a short film at motionpoems.com.

Thank you to my husband, Noah, and my son, Aaron. Thank you to Kanye and Donda West. Thank you to Judy Michaels, Tom Quigley, Cathy Day, Tom Cable, Brian Bremen, Bruce Snider, and Marie Howe. And so thank you to Princeton Day School, The College of New Jersey, The University of Texas at Austin, and the Michener Center for Writers where I met these wonderful teachers.

Thank you to Todd Davis and Julia Kasdorf. If it hadn't been for Todd's support at the very start, who knows if I would've continued. If it weren't for Julia, this book wouldn't ask for or give or risk or trust nearly as much. And so thank you to The Pennsylvania State University where I met them.

Thank you to my friends—Lynne Beckenstein, Linda Gallant, and Rachel Mennies. Thank you to all the fans of Kanye West I've met along the way, especially my friend EJ Koh. Thank you to my husband's family. Thank you Mom, Dad, Nick, Victoria, and Bian. And Pop Pop, who I miss dearly.

Thank you to Wesleyan University Press and Suzanna Tamminen for believing in this book as a book. And special thanks to the National Endowment for the Arts.

Thank you, too, to Josiah Meekins, Sarah Yake, Evan McGarvey, Bronwyn Becker, Sheila Squillante, Geffrey Davis, Natalie Eilbert, Daniel Story, Kimberly Andrews, Lauren Tyrrell, Aaron Kimmel, Sarah RudeWalker, Alyse Bensel, Emily Anderson, Robin Becker, Elizabeth Kadetsky, Toni Jensen, and many others.

For everything, just everything, thank you to Catie Rosemurgy.

ABOUT THE AUTHOR

𝔖arah 𝔟lake received her MFA in creative writing from the Pennsylvania State University in 2011 and her MA in creative writing from the University of Texas at Austin in 2008. She is a recipient of a 2013 NEA Literature Fellowship. She lives near Philadelphia with her husband and son. An online reader's companion is available at sarahblake.site.wesleyan.edu.